Contents

Introduction

Developing the skills of counting and writing numbers to 5

The first steps for children learning to count often begin informally at home with their families. They hear and see numbers in their daily lives and start to rehearse counting by saying numbers in nursery rhymes, listening to stories such as 'The Three Bears' and watching programmes on television. They may also begin to experiment with counting when playing with their toys or when carrying out familiar tasks such as climbing the stairs at bedtime.

By the time they reach four years of age, children of average ability and above are starting to draw pictures or marks on paper which represent numbers of objects. This may be a simple circle with two dots and two 'sticks' at the bottom of the circle representing a person, or a group of basic shapes or marks representing different objects.

Numbers to 5 acknowledges these developments and endeavours to provide a structured programme for children who are at the stage of rehearsing counting to five (or more) and are showing signs of being able to represent numbers through marks, pictures or written numbers on paper.

This book focuses on the next step in children's development. It aims to help children to develop confidence in counting up to five with all sorts of objects in different situations, to associate the counting process with written numbers and to encourage children to recognize and practise writing numbers. It also introduces

children to placing written numbers in the correct order and the first principles of addition – adding one more object to a small group and then counting to find the total.

Early Learning Goals

Numbers to 5 is for children who are at the beginning stages of counting and writing numbers, and who are using numbers in practical contexts to solve simple problems which involve counting.

This book provides a programme that helps children towards achieving the following Early Learning Goals for Mathematics identified by the Qualifications and Curriculum Authority (QCA):
- Say and use number names in order in familiar contexts.
- Count reliably up to 10 everyday objects.
- Recognize numerals 1 to 9.
- Find one more or one less than a number from 1 to 10.
- Begin to relate addition to combining two groups of objects, and subtraction to 'taking away'.
- Use developing mathematical ideas and methods to solve practical problems.

Baseline Assessment

The activities in this book are planned to develop mathematical skills in young children that will help them to confidently tackle the Baseline Assessment Tasks that they will be expected to carry out when they enter Reception classes in mainstream schools.

How to use this book

The activities in this book are designed to be used flexibly according to the children's level of development. While there is a planned structure to the activities for four-year-olds, there is also consideration given to younger and older children. The activities are specifically designed to help children to develop skills when working with numbers up to five. There are structured activities that include practical group and individual tasks, games focusing on each of the numbers 1 to 5 and photocopiable sheets to help children develop and consolidate their skills. Where the photocopiable sheet is to be used by individual children, it is referred to as an 'Individual recording' and can be kept for assessment purposes. If the sheet is to be used by a group of children, then it is referred to as an 'Individual task'. All the activities are adult-directed and require the presence and interaction of an adult.

The Skills development chart at the back of the book is designed to help you to incorporate the activities in your planning procedures. Ensure that adult helpers are pre-briefed about the activities and the preparation that needs to be carried out beforehand.

Progression

The practical activities in *Numbers to 5* introduce each number in turn, enabling children to explore each number and to practise counting and writing numbers. Activities are also provided for children to solve simple problems in practical contexts with numbers to 5 leading to the principle of adding one more to a small group of objects and counting to find the total number. For additional work, you may wish to use the second book in the series *Numbers to 10*, which focuses on developing children's confidence and understanding of numbers to 10 and beyond.

Finding out what children know beforehand

Before you begin to plan your work, it is helpful to find out what the children already know. You can achieve this by:
● checking how far a child can count orally
● finding out how far a child can count objects correctly by touching them and saying the number
● checking how far the child can write numbers in a recognizable form
● finding out how many objects a child can count by sight without touching them
● counting out a small set of objects with a child, then adding one or two objects. Does the child tell you the number by counting the objects or is he able to work it out mentally?
● counting out a small set of objects with a child, then taking one or two objects away. Does the child tell you the number by counting the objects or is he able to work it out mentally?
Note: The above suggestions are developmental and will not necessarily be appropriate for all children. It is up to you to decide which suggestions you should use. If a child can confidently carry out all of the above, and can count and write numbers above 5, then you may prefer to use the activities in the second book in the series, *Numbers to 10*.

Home links

Each activity includes suggestions to encourage parents and carers to help their child at home. If you wish to involve parents, it is important to establish this principle at the beginning and ensure that they receive appropriate guidance. This can be achieved informally through daily contact. If you are concerned about a particular child, and wish the child's parents to help with a specific skill, it is important that you share your ideas with them and invite their observations.

All about one

Learning objectives
To recognize the numeral 1; to trace numbers and words and draw one object.

Group size
Four to six children working with an adult.

What you need
A copy of the photocopiable sheet for each child; a card showing a large number 1; a tray of different small toys; pasta shapes; glue; pencils and crayons.

What to do
Invite the children to sit around a table and place the tray of toys in the middle of the table. Start by showing the number card to the children and talking about the number 1. Ask the children to hold up one finger. Now ask the children to look at the selection of toys on the tray. Ask them in turn to choose just one toy from the tray, and to tell you what they have taken.

Individual recording
Show the children how to draw the number 1 in the air, drawing a straight line from top to bottom, and ask them to copy your movements. Repeat this several times. Now ask the children to trace the dotted number 1s on the top of the photocopiable sheet. Show them how to form the number correctly, placing their pencil on the dot to start, and writing in the direction of the arrow. Now ask the children to draw a colourful picture of one object in the space on the sheet. This could be a toy, an animal or even themselves. Let them decorate the outline of the number 1 by sticking on pasta shapes. To finish, encourage the children to trace over the dotted

'one' words starting at the big dots each time and following the arrows.

Make the completed sheets into a group book with the title 'All about one'. Select one of the sheets and mount it onto card to start a group wall frieze. Alternatively, mount the sheets onto card, and keep them, taped together with the other 'All about ...' sheets, to make individual zigzag books showing the numbers 1 to 5 or a wall frieze for the children to take home.

Support
Cut off the section on the sheet showing the outline of the number 1 and let the children make the pasta picture or decorate the shape using coloured pens and pencils. Keep the sheets and tape them together with the outline of the other numbers presented later in the book, to make a wall frieze of the numbers 1 to 5.

Extension
Scribe the number and the name of the object below the children's picture for them to copy underneath.

Assessment
Note whether the child can trace the numbers and words correctly and whether she has been able to draw one object to match the number.

Home links
Give parents a prepared sheet and ask them to help their child to practise tracing and writing number 1s and drawing one object. Ask them to look for examples of the number 1 on car number plates or in shops when they are out and about with their child.

All about one

one

Weather watch

Learning objectives
To count using tally marks and to match pictures of objects with counters.

Group size
Whole group activity followed by a game for two to four children working with an adult.

What you need
Three copies of the photocopiable sheet; large sheet of thick card; three A4 sheets of thin card; laminating materials; a water-based marker; felt-tipped pens; large dice or cube; four sets of six counters of the same colour; glue.

Preparation
Draw a weather chart on the large sheet of thick card and laminate. Colour the suns and umbrellas on each copy of the photocopiable sheet, or invite the children to colour them. Glue the sheets onto thin card and laminate two of them. Cut the two laminated cards along the thick black lines to make four playing boards (two cards with six suns and two with six umbrellas). Make a picture dice by cutting out three of the suns and three of the umbrellas from the third sheet and sticking them onto the sides of a large cube or dice.

What to do
Position the prepared weather chart where all the children can see it. Talk about the weather today. Is it sunny, cloudy or rainy? Invite one child to draw a 1 or 'tally mark' in the correct row on the chart with a water-based marker. Do this every day for a week. Each day, ask the children to count with you as you point to each of the tally marks in each row.

At the end of the week, count the marks in each row with the children and write the total

number in the box. Talk about the results. Have there been more sunny days than rainy days? Which row has the most number of marks? Which has the least number of marks? Do any rows have the same number of marks?

Individual task
Give each child a playing board with either suns or umbrellas on, and a set of six counters of the same colour. Show the children the picture dice and explain that they must take turns to throw the dice. If a child with a sun card throws a 'sun', then he can place a counter on the first sun on his board. If he throws an 'umbrella', then he must pass the dice on to the next player. The first child to place all six counters on his or her card is declared the winner.

Support
Keep a record of the weather for one week at a time. Wipe the board at the end of each week.

Extension
Keep a record of the weather for two weeks. Ask the children to count the number of marks in the rows and invite a child to write the numbers in the boxes at the end of the rows each day with a water-based marker. Wipe off the numbers in the boxes before each session.

Assessment
Note whether the child can record using tally marks and count the total. Is he able to identify the rows with the most/least/same number of tally marks?

Home links
Ask parents to help their child practise tallying at home by letting him lay the table at mealtimes, matching one knife and one fork to each place.

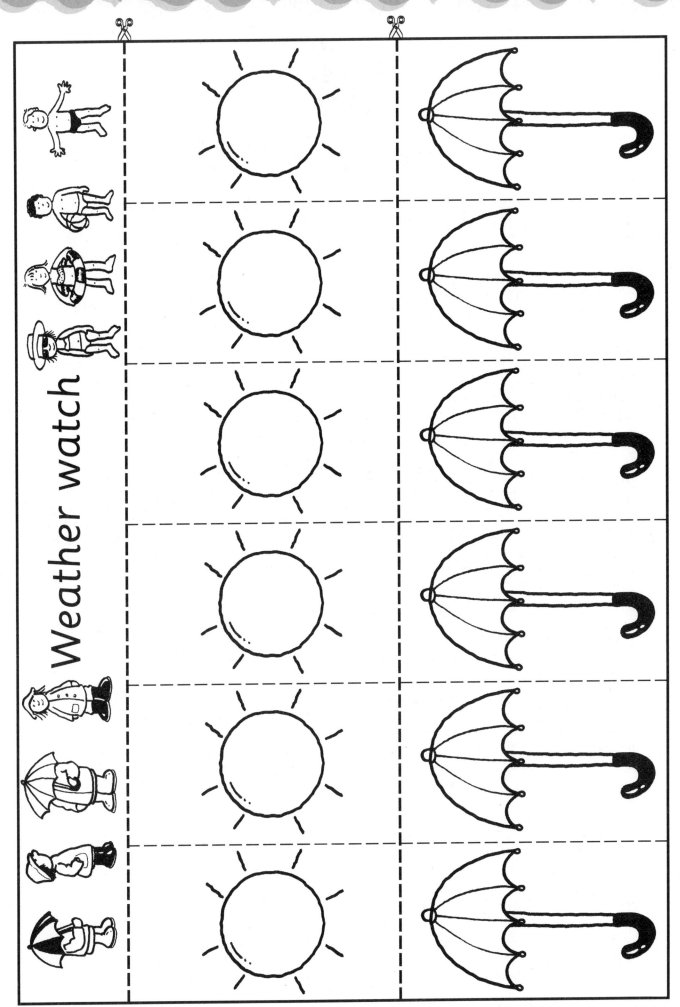

Choose a pair

Learning objectives
To recognize the numeral 2; to trace numbers and words and draw two objects.

Group size
Four to six children working with an adult.

What you need
A copy of the photocopiable sheet for each child; a card showing a large number 2; two tables; pairs of shoes and gloves of different sizes; coloured tissue paper; glue; pencils and crayons.

Preparation
Set the gloves and shoes out on two tables in front of the group, putting one of each pair on each table.

What to do
Sit the children in front of the tables and show them the large number card.
Talk about the number 2, and ask the children to hold up two fingers. Ask one child to choose a shoe or glove, then to look on the other table to find the matching shoe or glove. Repeat until each child has a pair, then ask them in turn to tell you what they have taken, for example, 'a pair of red wellingtons'. Invite the children to put one of each pair back on each table, then repeat the activity to find a different pair. Ask how many gloves or shoes each child has, for example, 'I have got two blue gloves'.

Finish the activity by asking individual children to say how many eyes, ears, feet, arms and legs they have (include noses, heads and chins to vary the counting).

Individual recording
Show the children how to draw the number 2 in the air. Talk them through the movements and ask them to copy you. Now ask them to trace the dotted 2s on the top of the sheet, starting at the big dot and following the arrows. Invite the children to decorate the outline of the number 2 by sticking on scrunched-up or ripped-up pieces of tissue paper, then let them draw two objects in the empty space next to it. Finish the activity by tracing over the dotted 'two' words starting at the big dots and following the arrows.

Make the completed sheets into a group book with the title 'All about two'. Select one of the sheets and mount it onto card to continue the group wall frieze.

Alternatively, mount the sheets onto card and tape them together with the 'All about one' sheets to make individual zigzag books 1 to 5 or a wall frieze for the children to take home.

Support
Cut off the section showing the outline of the number 2 and let the children make the tissue-paper picture.

Extension
Ask the children to count all of the shoes and gloves on the tables. Scribe the number and the name of the objects below the children's drawings for them to copy underneath.

Assessment
Note whether the child can match the pairs of shoes and gloves correctly, whether she can trace the numbers and words correctly and draw two objects to match the number.

Home links
Ask parents to let their child help pair up socks or shoes at home. Give parents a prepared sheet for the child to practise tracing and writing the number 2 and drawing two objects.

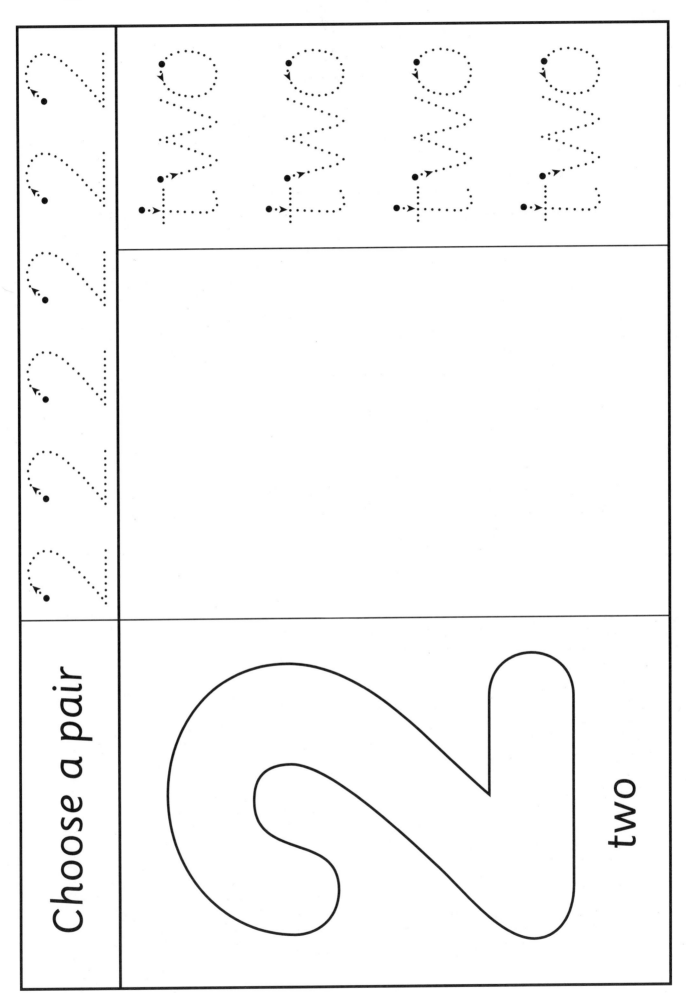

Choose a pair

two

Icing biscuits

Learning objectives
To practise counting sets of two objects by decorating biscuits with two sweets; to tally sets of two with counters.

Group size
Two to four children working with an adult.

What you need
For the biscuits: Plain biscuits; small jelly sweets; small packet of icing sugar or ready-mixed icing; table knives; a sieve; a mixing bowl; a jug of warm boiled water; a dinner plate; clean aprons.
For the game: Four copies of the photocopiable sheet; four sets of ten coloured counters; thin card; laminating materials; a dice; three large adhesive coloured spots.

Preparation
Biscuits: To prepare the icing, sift 100g (4oz) of icing sugar into the mixing bowl. Add 15ml (1tbsp) of warm water or sufficient to make the icing thick enough to coat the back of a spoon. This will make enough icing for 12 biscuits. Place the biscuits and jelly sweets on a plate.
Game: Laminate four copies of the photocopiable sheet to make playing boards. Stick adhesive spots to three sides of the dice.

What to do
Ask the children to wash their hands and put on clean aprons. Invite them to each take a biscuit from the plate, and to spread a thin layer of icing over one side of their biscuit. Now ask the children in turn to choose two jelly sweets. Encourage them to use the sweets to decorate their biscuit. Put the biscuits on the plate and leave to set. Give children an opportunity to count the biscuits and the sweets at the end of the activity. Repeat so that all children have a turn to ice and decorate a biscuit.

Individual task
Give each child a playing board and a set of ten counters of one colour. Show the children the 'spot' dice and explain that they must take turns to throw the dice. If a child throws a 'spot' then he can put a counter on top of a 'sweet' on one of the biscuits on the plate. If he throws a 'blank' (number) then they cannot place a counter, and must pass the dice on to the next player. The first child to place two counters on each of their five biscuits is the winner.

Support
Play the game where the children put two counters on each biscuit if they throw a 'spot'.

Extension
Play the game with two 'spot' dice, giving the children the chance to throw two spots, one spot or two blanks. Encourage them to add the spots together to work out how many counters to place on their biscuit.

Assessment
Note whether the child can play the game correctly. Can he count the number of decorated biscuits and the number of sweets correctly? Does he count the sweets on the biscuits in ones or can he count them in twos?

Home links
Give parents a copy of the ingredients and the method and encourage them to help their child ice and decorate some biscuits at home.

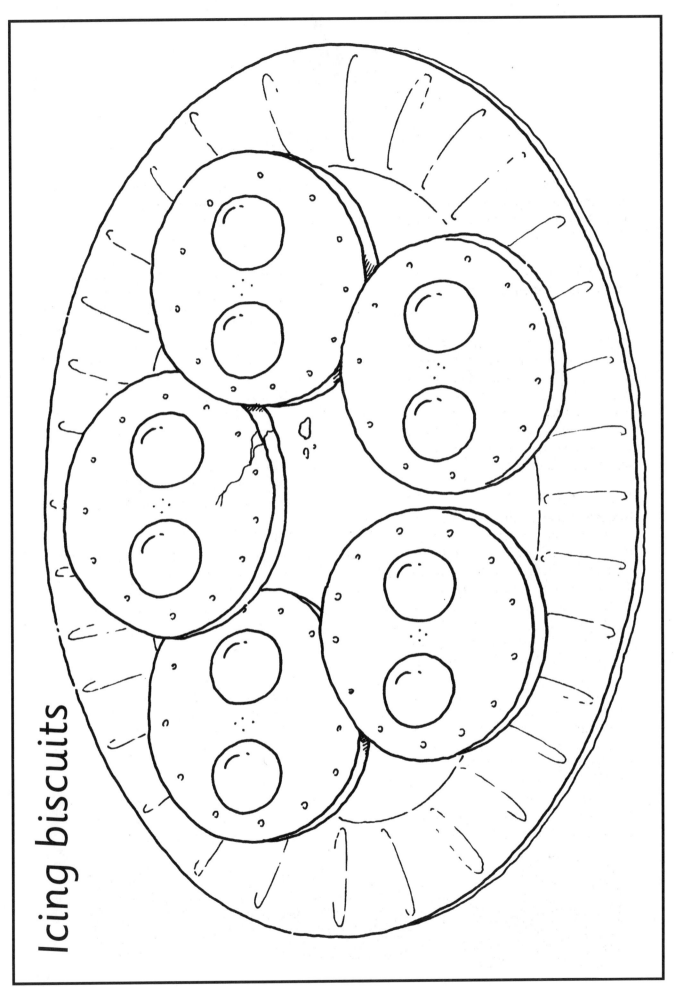

Icing biscuits

Count to three

Learning objectives
To recognize the numeral 3; to trace numbers and words and draw three objects.

Group size
Four to six children working with an adult.

What you need
A copy of the activity sheet for each child; a card showing a large number 3; an assorted collection of sets of three small objects in a tray, for example cars, Lego bricks or play people; six paper plates; small buttons or sequins; glue; pencils and crayons.

What to do
Sit the children at a table and put the tray of objects in the centre. Show them the large number card and talk about the number 3. Ask the children to count aloud to three, first together and then individually, and to hold up three fingers. Give each child a paper plate. Ask them in turn to find a set of three objects from the tray and put them on their plate. Ask them to say what they have taken, for example 'three cars'. Now ask each child in turn to put one object back and to say how many are left until there are no more objects on the plates

Repeat the activity, asking children to take one object each time and to say how many they have on their plates. Encourage the children to choose a different set of three objects.

Individual recording
Show the children how to draw the number 3 in the air. Talk them through the movements and ask them to copy you. Now ask them to trace the dotted number 3s at the top of their sheet, placing their pencil on the big dot to start.

Show them the sequins and buttons, and invite them to stick these onto the sheet to fill the outline of the number 3. Now ask the children to draw a set of three objects in the space. Finish by tracing over the dotted 'three' words starting at the big dots each time.

Make the sheets into a group book with the title 'All about three'. Mount one of the sheets onto card to continue the wall frieze or tape together with the other 'All about ...' sheets, to make zigzag books for the numbers 1 to 5.

Support
Cut off the section with the outline of the number three and let the children make a button/sequin picture. Tape the sheets together with the outlines of other numbers to make a wall frieze.

Extension
Ask the children to put three different objects on their plate each time, and to count the objects out loud. Now ask them to count the number of plates on the table. How many objects are there on two plates? How many on three plates? Scribe the number and the name of the objects the children have drawn on their activity sheet for them to copy underneath.

Assessment
Note whether the child can choose a set of three objects correctly. Can she trace the numbers and words correctly? Is she able to draw a set of three objects to match the number?

Home links
Give parents a prepared sheet to use with their child at home. Ask them to look for examples of the number 3 around the house, for example on clocks or on digital displays.

Count to three

three

Three bears

Learning objective
To sort and match sets of three objects related by size.

Group size
Whole group game followed by small group activity for four to six children working with an adult.

What you need
Whole group game:
A safe, open space; three different-sized teddies, bowls and spoons; three chairs.
Small group activity:
A copy of the photocopiable sheet for each child; scissors; glue and crayons.

Preparation
Cut the strip of bears, bowls and spoons from each sheet.

What to do
Place three chairs in a line and sit the children in front of the chairs. Give the three bears, bowls and spoons to different children. Choose a child to be 'Golidlocks'.

Ask the children with the bowls to put them down in front of the chairs starting with the big bowl, then the middle-sized bowl, then the small bowl. Say the rhyme with the children, as Goldilocks holds up each bowl in turn:

When Goldilocks went to the house of the bears, what did her blue eyes see?
A bowl that was HUGE, a bowl that was small and a bowl that was tiny and that was all,
She counted them *one, two, three.*

Now ask the children with the spoons to put them in the correct-sized bowl. Say the rhyme again, substituting the word 'bowl' with 'spoon'. This time Goldilocks holds up each spoon and counts them in the same way as the bowls. Ask the children holding the bears to sit on the correct chair. Say the rhyme again, and this time the children holding the bears should hold up their bear at the appropriate point.

Repeat the game, giving the bears, bowls and spoons to different children and choosing another child to be 'Goldilocks'.

Individual recording
Give each child a pair of scissors. Invite them to colour the pictures on the sheet, then to cut along the dotted lines to separate them. In the first column, ask the children to stick the big bear in the top square, the big bowl in the middle square and the big spoon in the bottom square. Stick the bowls into the second column in the same way, and the spoons in the third. As they work, encourage the children to explain what they are doing, using comparative language such as 'bigger than'.

Support
Help the children to lay the items in the correct squares before they stick them onto the sheet.

Extension
When the children have completed the sheet, ask them to count how many items there are altogether.

Assessment
Check whether the child can match the bears, bowls and spoons correctly in relation to size.

Home links
Encourage parents to read or tell their child the story of 'The Three Bears' at bedtime. Ask them to count the sets of three items with their child.

Three bears

Find the number four

Learning objectives
To recognize the numeral 4; to trace numbers and words and draw four objects.

Group size
Four to six children working with an adult.

What you need
A copy of the photocopiable sheet for each child; a table; a card showing a large number 4; a collection of objects showing the number 4, such as birthday cards, dice, playing cards and a calendar; magazines; glue; pencils and crayons.

Preparation
Display the collection of 'four' objects on the table. Cut the pages of the magazines into small squares (approximately 2cm x 2cm).

What to do
Start by showing the large number card to the children. Ask them to tell you what number it is and to hold up the same number of fingers. Ask the children to count aloud to four, first together and then individually. Ask the children in turn to take one item from the display table. Help them to find the example of the number 4 on the object, and to show the number to the rest of the group.

Individual recording
Demonstrate to the children how to draw the number 4 in the air with your finger, and ask them to copy you as you talk them through the movements. Repeat this several times. Now ask them to trace the dotted number 4s in pencil on the top of the photocopiable sheet, starting at the big dot each time and writing in the direction of the arrows.

Show the children the magazine squares and invite them to fill in the outline of the number 4 by sticking and overlapping the squares onto the shape. When they have filled the outline, ask them to draw a set of four objects in the space. Encourage the children to complete the sheet by tracing over the dotted 'four' words, starting at the big dots each time and following the arrows.

Secure the completed sheets together to make a group book with the title 'All about four'. Continue the group wall frieze, adding one of the sheets mounted onto card. Alternatively, mount all the sheets onto card and tape them together with the children's other 'All about ...' sheets to make individual zigzag books or wall friezes.

Support
Cut off the section showing the outline of the number 4. Encourage the children to make a colourful picture by filling the outline with the paper squares. Tape the sheets together with the other number pictures to make a wall frieze.

Extension
Scribe the number and the name of the objects below the picture they have drawn for them to copy underneath.

Assessment
Note whether the child can trace the numbers and words correctly and whether he is able to draw four objects to match the number.

Home links
Give parents a prepared sheet to use at home with their child. Ask them to look out for sets of four with their child, such as wheels on cars or windows on houses.

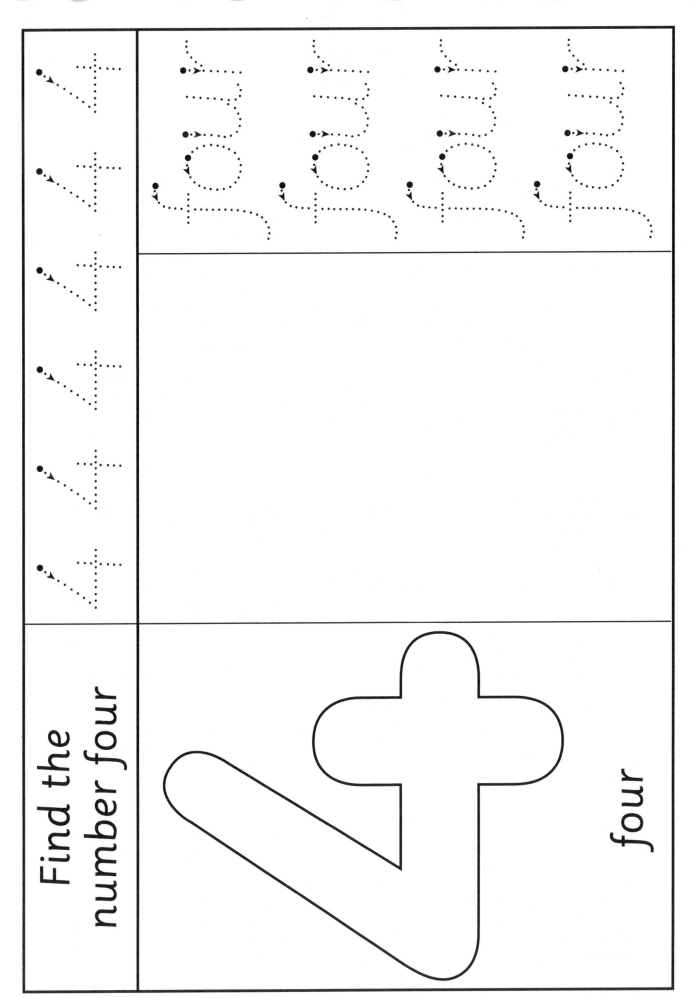

Find the number four

four

Moneybags

Learning objectives
To practise counting to four; to tally sets of four using coins.

Group size
Four children working with an adult.

What you need
For the activity: Four small clear plastic bank bags, each with four pennies in; four paper plates labelled 1p, 2p, 3p, 4p; four different small toys.
For the game: Four copies of the activity sheet copied onto thin card; laminating materials; a cube or dice with the numbers 1–6 replaced by 1p, 2p, 3p, 1p, 2p, 3p; a small tray containing 1p coins.

Preparation
Laminate the four copies of the photocopiable sheet to make four playing boards.

What to do
Sit the children around a table and place the four plates with a small toy on each in the centre. Give each child a money bag containing four 1p coins. Ask each child in turn to choose one of the toys to buy and pay for using the pennies in their money bag. Ask them to put the correct amount of coins on the plate and take the toy. Ask 'How much does it cost?' and 'How much money do you have left in your bag?'

When all the children have bought a toy, count the money on each plate with the children. Put all the money in the centre of the table and, in turn, ask the children to take the correct number of 1p coins so that they each have four coins in their bags. Check that all the bags are correct then repeat the activity asking the children to choose a different toy to buy.

Individual task
Let the children work in groups of two to four to play a tally game. Give each child a Moneybags board and place the tray of 1p coins in the centre of the table. Explain to the children that they have to take turns to throw the dice. If they throw a 2p, they should take two coins from the tray and place each of them on a coin outline on their board. The first player to fill all four money bags with four coins calls out 'Moneybags!' and is declared the winner.

Support
Use the Moneybags boards for children to match the outlines of coins in the bags with 1p coins. Count the number of coins in each bag.

Extension
Play the Moneybags game backwards. The children should start by putting 1p coins on all of the coin outlines on the board. When they throw the dice, they have to take off that number of coins each time. The first child with no coins left calls out 'Broke!' and is declared the winner. Make the game more challenging by having a rule that the child must throw the exact number to finish. (Vary the game by playing with £1 coins.)

Assessment
Check that the child can count out amounts up to 4p. Can she count how many coins she has left in her bag and add more coins to make 4p?

Home links
Encourage parents to help their child at home by letting her sort out all the 1p coins or £1 coins from a purse at different times and count how much money altogether.

Moneybags

Fill in five

Learning objectives
To recognize the numeral 5; to trace numbers and words and draw five objects.

Group size
Four to six children working with an adult.

What you need
A copy of the activity sheet for each child; a card showing a large number 5; a paint tray with sponges soaked in different-coloured paints; printing sticks (1cm doweling cut into short lengths); pencils; crayons.

What to do
Show the large number card to the children and talk about the number 5. Ask them to join in as you count up to five together. Can they show you five fingers? Sing some action rhymes such as 'Five currant buns', 'Five little peas' or 'Five little ducks' which can be found in *This Little Puffin* compiled by Elizabeth Matterson (Puffin) – and invite the children to join in the actions with you.

Individual recording
Show the children how to draw a large number 5 in the air. Talk them through the movements and invite them to copy you. Now ask them to trace the dotted number 5s on the top of the sheet, placing their pencil on the big dot to start, and writing in the direction of the arrows.

Tell the children that they are going to make a picture of the number 5 by printing some colourful shapes. Give each child a short length of 1cm doweling and, on a separate sheet of paper, demonstrate how to press the doweling onto one of the paint-soaked sponges then onto the paper to make a printed shape. Invite the

children to do the same using the different-coloured paint, until they have filled the outline of the number 5 on their sheet.

Invite the children to place their hand in the space on the sheet and to draw around it, counting their fingers as they draw around each one. Finish by asking the children to trace over the dotted 'five' words, starting at the big dots each time and following the arrows.

Use the completed sheets to make a group number book with the title 'All about five'. Select one sheet and mount it onto card to continue the group wall frieze. Alternatively, mount all the sheets onto card and tape them together with the other 'All about ...' sheets to make individual zigzag books or a wall frieze for the children to take home.

Support
Cut off the section showing the number outline and let the children print a shape picture. Tape the sheets together with the other number pictures to continue the wall frieze.

Extension
Scribe the numbers 1 to 5 on the children's hand tracings for them to copy. Can they tell you how many fingers there are on two hands?

Assessment
Note whether the child can trace the numbers and words correctly and whether he can count to five on his fingers.

Home links
Encourage parents to help their children at home by giving them a prepared sheet for the child to practise tracing and writing the number 5 and drawing five objects.

Fill in five

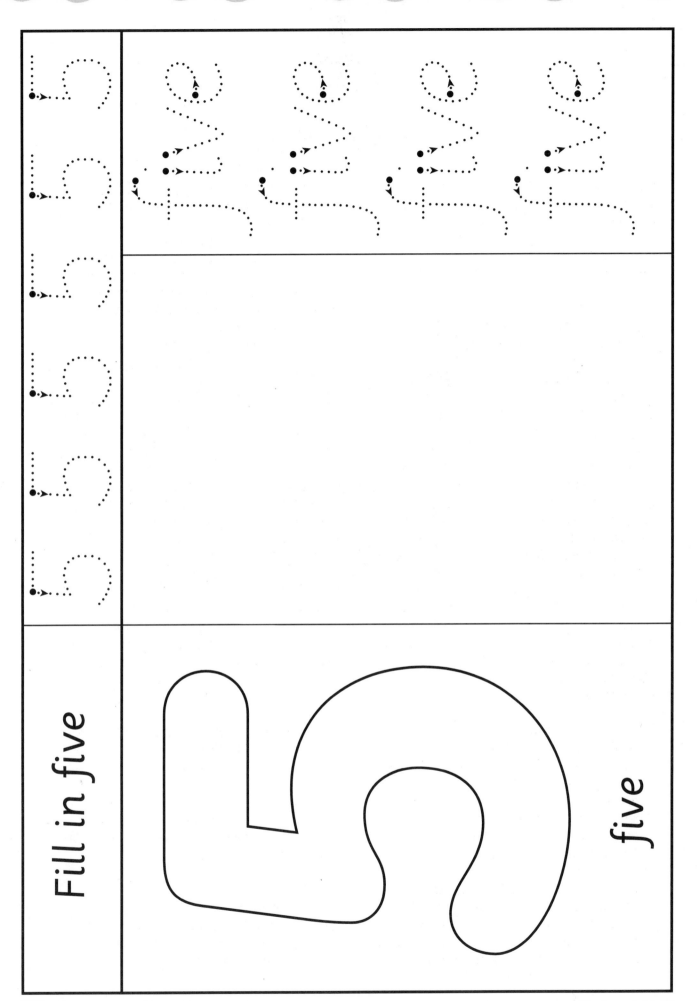

five

Fish pond

Learning objective
To practise counting and writing numbers to five.

Group size
Three to five children working with an adult.

What you need
A copy of the photocopiable sheet for each child and one for the adult; thin card; laminating materials; a tray; sets of five objects, such as toy cars or animals; crayons or felt-tipped pens; glue; scissors; a copy of the rhyme 'One, two, three, four, five, Once I caught a fish alive', from *This Little Puffin* compiled by Elizabeth Matterson (Puffin).

Preparation
Cut the strips of fish from each activity sheet. Stick your sheet to thin card. Colour each fish a different colour, laminate the card, then cut the individual fish cards out. Photocopy extra strips of fish for older children.

What to do
Place the tray of objects in the middle of the table. Ask each child to take one set of objects from the tray and to count the number of objects out loud. When each child has had a turn, change the number of objects in the tray by removing some, so that some sets have three or four objects. Repeat the activity several times, changing the numbers of objects each time.

Now introduce the song 'One, two, three, four five, Once I caught a fish alive'. Sing this a few times, encouraging the children to join in. Place your photocopiable sheet in the centre of the table and give each child a laminated fish card. Ask them in turn to put their fish in the pond, asking each time, 'How many fish are in the pond now?' Repeat a few times, changing the order of the children placing the fish.

Individual recording
Ask the children to trace over the numbers on their photocopiable sheet with a pencil, starting from the big dots and following the outline. Let them colour in the pond. Next, ask them to colour the strip of fish, and then help them to cut along the dotted lines to separate the fish. Ask the children to stick their fish in the pond on the sheet. Ask them to count the number of fish in the pond and write the number in the box.

Support
Reduce the number of fish according to the number of objects the children can count by touching. Write the number in the box in yellow marker for the children to trace.

Extension
Increase the number of objects in the tray according to the number of objects the children can count by touching. Increase the number of fish to the number of objects the children can count by touching. Prepare a sheet with a larger pond to accommodate the extra fish.

Assessment
Note whether the child needs to count the fish by touching them or whether she can count them by sight. Check that the child can write the number of fish correctly by tracing, copying or from memory.

Home links
Encourage parents to help their child count the number of bath toys at bathtime.

Fish pond

Number plates

Learning objectives
To recognize zero and to match objects to numbers one to five.

Group size
Four to six children working with an adult.

What you need
A copy of the photocopiable sheet for each child; six paper plates numbered 0–5; a tray of sets of small countable objects; small cubes or printing sticks; paint tray with sponges soaked in different-coloured paint.

Preparation
Write the numbers 0–5 in the boxes on the sheet in random order.

What to do
Sit the children around a table and place the tray of countable objects in the centre of the table. Give each child a paper plate and ask them in turn to take a set of objects from the tray that matches the number on their plate. Count the objects with the children to make sure they have taken the correct number. When all the children have had a turn, collect in the plates and objects, then give them out again making sure that each child has a different plate. Repeat the activity a few times.

Individual recording
Give each child a small cube or printing stick and place the paint tray in the centre of the table. Ask the children to print the correct number of cubes/shapes on each plate on their sheet to match the numbers in the boxes.

Support
Use two sets of plates numbered 1–3 for the group activity. Write the numbers 1–3 in random order in the boxes on the sheet.

Extension
Use a set of six plates numbered 2–8 or 4–10 for the group activity. Alternatively, use a set of ten plates numbered 1–10. Write numbers on the photocopiable sheet in random order that relate to the numbers used in the group activity.

Assessment
Check that the child can match objects to numbers correctly.

Home links
Invite parents to help their child at home by using a pack of playing cards. Tell them to sort out all the cards from aces to fives, and spread them out face up on a table. Ask them to help their child sort the cards into number piles, for example, all the aces, all the twos and so on.

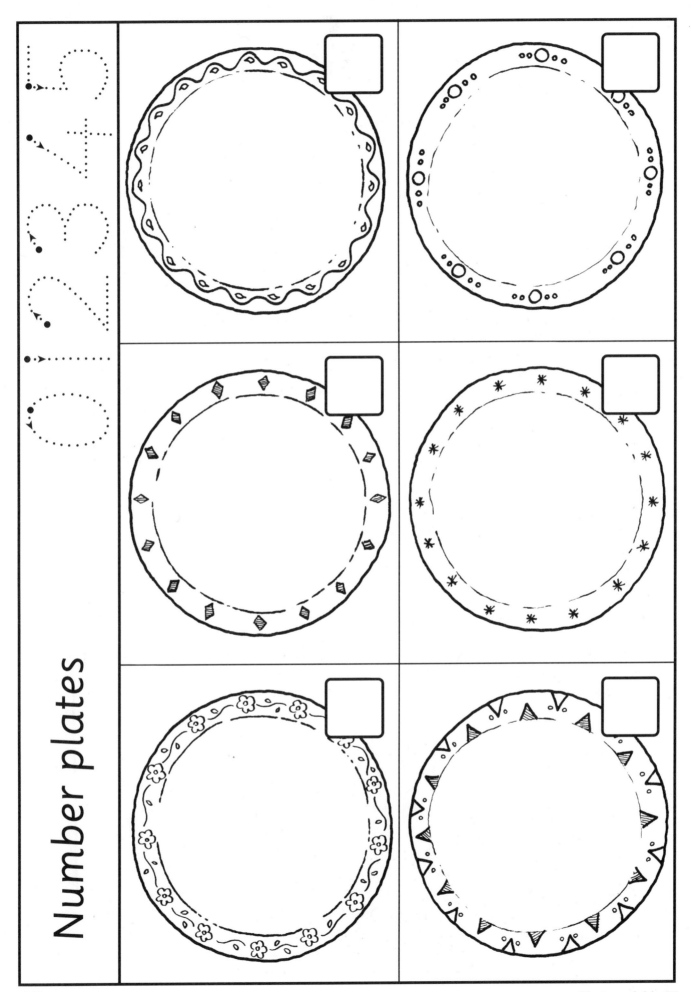

Number plates

Collect a set

Learning objective
To recognize that any collection of five objects will have five members.

Group size
Four to six children working with an adult.

What you need
A copy of the activity sheet for each child; six paper plates; a large tray; crayons or felt-tipped pens; paper; paint and brushes; a yellow marker.

What to do
Place the tray in the centre of the table and give a paper plate to each child. Ask them to collect a set of five small objects from around the room on their plate and bring the set back to the group. You can leave the choice of objects open to the children or specify one criterion, for example 'yellow things' or 'shiny things'. When the children return to the group ask them to put their plate in front of them. Ask each child to count the objects on their plate and to describe their collection. When the children have completed this, ask them to put their objects in the empty tray. Ask the children if they can make other sets from the collection, such as all the round objects, and count the objects.

Individual recording
Ask the children to draw five different flowers in the window box on their sheet using crayons or felt-tipped pens. When they have finished, give the children a blank sheet of paper each and ask them to paint a vase holding five different flowers. Use the pictures to create a wall display.

Support
Reduce the number of objects that the children have to collect and the number of flowers to be drawn in the window boxes to a number that each child can confidently count and recognize.

Extension
Increase the number of objects that the children have to collect and the number of flowers to be drawn in the window boxes to a number that each child can confidently count and recognize.

Assessment
Note whether the child can find five objects to make a set. Check that he has drawn five different flowers on the photocopiable sheet.

Home links
Ask parents to help their child count sets of objects such as five pieces of cutlery or fruit.

1 2 3 4 5

Collect a set

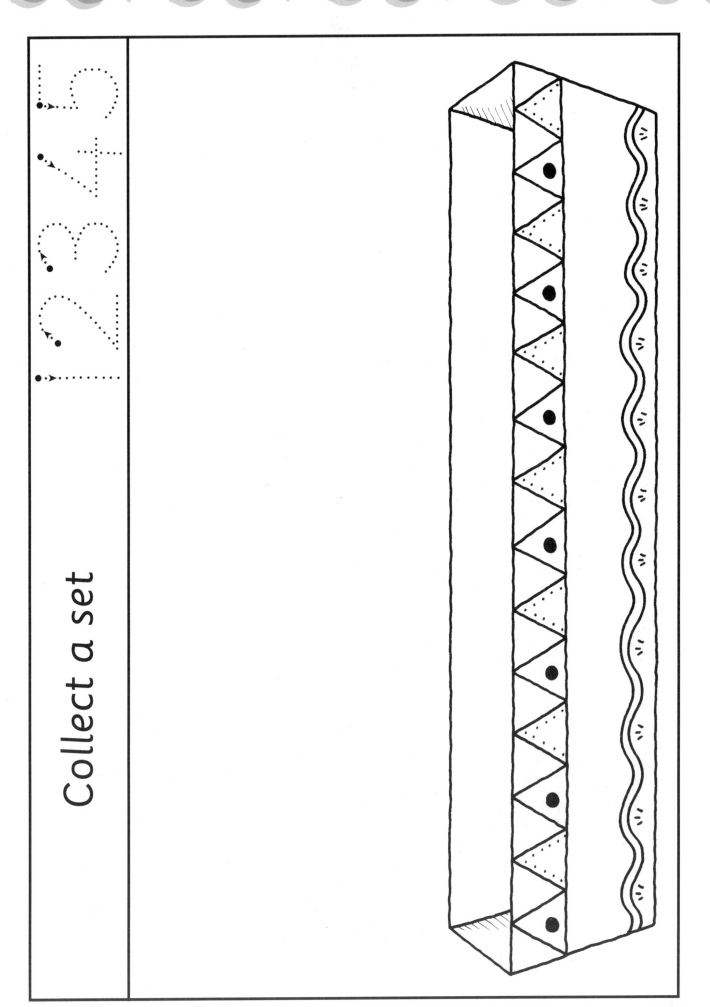

Washing line

Learning objectives
To practise recognizing written numbers one to five by sight and to place written numbers in the correct order.

Group size
Five children.

What you need
A copy of the photocopiable sheet for each child; a skipping rope; five clothes pegs; five large cards numbered 1–5; scissors; glue; crayons or felt-tipped pens.

Preparation
Cut the strips of numbered T-shirts off the bottom of the photocopiable sheets.

What to do
Tie the rope between two stable pieces of furniture at a height where the children can reach the rope easily. Sit the children in a space in front of the rope and yourself on a chair beside the rope. Start by holding up each of the large numbered cards in order and asking the children to say the numbers. Shuffle the cards and repeat the activity. Give a card and a peg to each child. Ask 'Who has the number one?'. Invite that child to peg their card on the line. Repeat for the number two and carry on until all the children have pegged their card on the line. Next, invite the children in turn to take a different card off the line. Collect in the cards and pegs and repeat a few times.

Now tell the children that you are going to hide one card. Peg the remaining four cards on the line in order, leaving a space for the hidden card. Ask a child to tell you the number of the hidden card and invite one child to peg the card in the right place on the line. Make sure that each child has at least one turn.

Individual recording
Ask the children to colour in the T-shirts on their photocopiable sheet, then to cut along the dotted lines so that they have five separate shirts. Ask them to stick the T-shirts on the washing line on the photocopiable sheet in the right order starting from the number one.

Support
Cut up the numbered T-shirts beforehand and give the children T-shirts to the number they can confidently count and recognize. Ask them to colour and stick them on the line in the right order.

Extension
In the oral washing line activity include cards numbered from 6–10 in the set, or up to an appropriate number in between. In the recording activity, ask the children to stick the T-shirts on the line in reverse order, starting with the biggest number first.

Assessment
Note whether the child is able to recognize written numbers one to five by sight and whether he can place the written numbers in the correct order.

Home links
Encourage parents to help their child at home by laying out aces to fives of one suit of playing cards in a line on a table and making a shuffled pile of the other three suit's aces to fives. The child can turn over a card and put it on top of a matching card until there are no cards left.

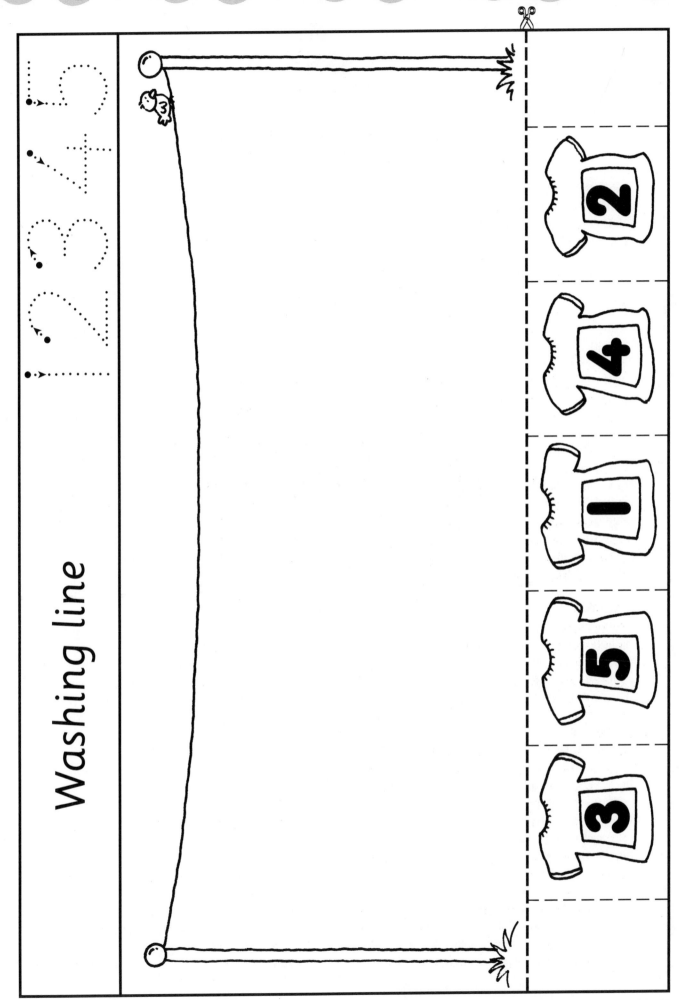

Washing line

Apple tree

Learning objective
To add one more object to a set by counting objects and then adding one more mentally.

Group size
Four to six children working with an adult.

What you need
A copy of the activity sheet for each child; large apple tree (see Preparation); at least five large red apples made from card; Blu-Tack; pencils; crayons or felt-tipped pens.

Preparation
Draw a large apple tree, approximately the same height as the children and attach to the wall. Stick Blu-Tack on the back of each cardboard apple.

What to do
Ask the children to sit on the floor in front of the apple tree picture. Stick a number of apples to the tree and ask the children to count them aloud. Ask them to tell you how many apples there are on the tree altogether. Invite one child to stick one more apple on the tree and then to tell you how many apples there are altogether. Do this several times so that all the children have a chance to count the apples, then remove all the apples from the tree.

Now, replace a number of apples and invite one child to count them. Ask the question, 'If there was one more apple on the tree, how many would there be?'. Make sure each child has a turn at counting and adding the apples.

Individual recording
Ask the children to colour the apples on the first tree on their photocopiable sheet. In the space, ask them to draw one more apple, and then count the total number of apples on the tree. Ask them to write the number of apples in the box beside the tree. Encourage them to do the same with the other apple trees on the sheet, adding one more apple each time and counting the total. When the children have finished, let them colour in the apple tree pictures.

Support
Invite the children to colour the apples on the tree, count them and write the number in the box. If they need help writing the number, draw the number with a yellow marker in the box for them to trace.

Extension
Increase the number of apples used in the oral activity and change the rule to adding two more apples each time. When the children complete the activity sheet, ask them to draw two more apples on each tree each time and write the number in the box.

As an alternative, take one apple away each time in the oral activity. When children complete the activity sheet, ask them to cross out one apple each time and write the number of apples left on the trees in the boxes.

Assessment
Check whether the child can add one more apple to the tree by touching or counting out loud all the apples or whether she is able to add more in her head.

Home links
Encourage parents to help their child at home by letting their child count small sets of fruit or vegetables, adding one more to the set or taking one away and counting the fruit each time.

Apple tree

Name _____

Skills development chart

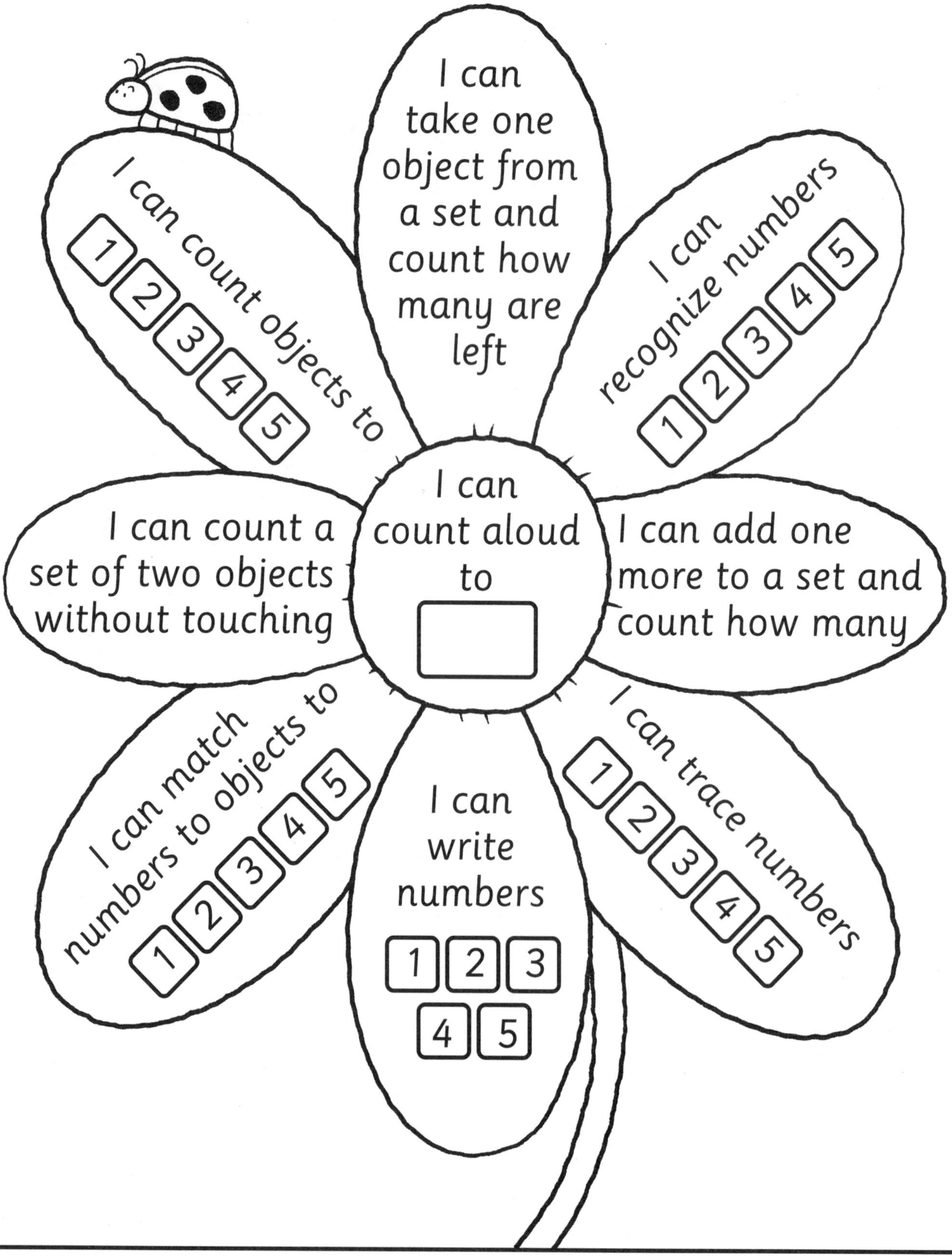

I can
take one
object from
a set and
count how
many are
left

I can count objects to
1 2 3 4 5

I can
recognize numbers
1 2 3 4 5

I can count a
set of two objects
without touching

I can
count aloud
to

I can add one
more to a set and
count how many

I can match
numbers to objects to
1 2 3 4 5

I can
write
numbers
1 2 3
4 5

I can trace numbers
1 2 3 4 5